Doggies

Don't Wear Sweaters

Doggies

Don't Wear Sweaters

WARE RESOURCES AND PUBLISHING
New York   Toronto   London
Sydney   Mexico City   New Delhi   Hong Kong

DOGGIES DON'T WEAR SWEATERS

Acknowledgements

To my neighbors' little 5-year-old son, who gave me the inspiration to write this children's book.

Wow, who would have thought that walking my "Brooklyn" would have sparked such a book! Thank you so much.

To my granddaughter Taylor, thank you for reading my story at the age of 10, encouraging me, saying, "Botchie, this is a good book!" I love you Taylor Dane.

In memory of my special friend, Charlie Driver," who has gone to test eternity, thank you for being the first "adult" to read my story and saying, "Hum Hum, this is a great children's book." I know he is smiling down on me.

To Sheila Warner, my supervisor, thank you for encouraging me to read this story to the day-care children. They loved it.

And to my sister-friends, Pasty, Dollie and family, thank you for keeping me encouraged and pushing me forward to achieve my goals.

And the best part of all, to my "Heavenly Father," thank you for giving me the talent, vision and tenacity even to consider becoming an author.

BOOK ONE

Doggies Don't Wear Sweaters

A pretty little silver Yorkie Poo doggie named Brooklyn lived with her mother in a big house. Brooklyn did not have any sisters or brothers, but she was never lonely. Brooklyn had a soft, beautiful bed to sleep in and lots of toys. She bounced and ran around the house, laughing and playing with her toys every day. Every evening and on the weekends, Brooklyn's mother would take her for a walk in the big park near their home. Brooklyn loved walking and playing with her friends in the park.

Beautiful **S**weaters

One of Brooklyn's favorite things to do was to wear pretty sweaters. Brooklyn's mother bought her sweaters of all colors with beautiful designs. Red, blue, green, orange, purple, silver, gold, brown, yellow, pink, white, dark blue, and gray, you name it, Brooklyn had a sweater in that color. Brooklyn had sweaters that she only wore in the house and sweaters that she only wore outside. She wore her outside sweaters in the springtime through early fall. Her favorite sweater was pink and white. Brooklyn only liked to wear this sweater on special occasions. It was a turtleneck sweater with pink and white diamond specs all over it. Brooklyn knew all of her doggie friends liked to see her prance around in her pretty sweater.

*T*he *B*irthday *P*arty

Brooklyn was invited to her friend Jax's birthday party in the big park. The party was on Saturday, the last day of spring. This was going to be a big day for Brooklyn. She asked her mommy if she could wear her pretty sweater with the pink and white diamond pattern. Her mommy said, "Yes." Brooklyn and her mommy went shopping for Jax's birthday gift. Her mommy bought Jax a Big bone tied in blue ribbon. Brooklyn was so excited that she could hardly wait for Saturday to come. The day of the party finally came. Brooklyn was so eager to get dressed that she forgot that she needed to have her silver hair brushed and her pink-and-white ribbons tied around her ears. After Brooklyn was dressed, she sat impatiently by the door waiting for her mommy to get ready. It seemed like it was taking her mommy a long time. Brooklyn kept saying, "Hurry up, Mommy, we are going to be late for the party!" Brooklyn wanted all of her friends to see her. She thought, "What in the world was taking Mommy so long?" Finally, Brooklyn's mommy was dressed, and they left to go to the party.

*T*O *T*HE

*P*ARTY

*W*E

*G*O!

On Their Way

As Brooklyn and her mommy were on their way, Brooklyn saw her friends Lou Lou and Barney. They were going to the party too. Lou Lou said, "Brooklyn, your sweater is simple adorable." Barney said, "It's OK for a girl's sweater." Brooklyn was so overjoyed to be strutting around in her beautiful sweater that she did not really care what the boys said about it. After all, Brooklyn knew that she would be the best-dressed girl doggie at the birthday party!

The Birthday Arrival

When Brooklyn and her mommy arrived, all the doggies was running and playing with balls and Frisbees. The park was decorated with beautiful balloons. Brooklyn looked for Jax in the crowded park. It must have been 20 doggies and their parents there. Then Brooklyn saw Jax standing next to his mother. Brooklyn ran over to him, her mommy following; Brooklyn said, "Hi, Jax, Happy Birthday! Here is your birthday gift." Jax loved the big bone tied in blue ribbon. He thanked Brooklyn and told her how pretty she looked in her sweater. Brooklyn said "thank you." It made her very happy to hear Jax say that.

The Birthday Arrival Continued

Next, Brooklyn ran to play games with the other birthday party guests. Brooklyn, Jax and the other doggies played for hours. Finally, they ate birthday cake and ice cream. Then it was time to go home. Brooklyn was very tired, but she had a lot of fun. She especially liked having everyone tell her that she was very pretty in her favorite sweater.

The Walk Home

As Brooklyn and her mommy were walking home, two little human boys were walking with their mother and father. The older boy said to his father, "Look, Daddy, at the doggie. The doggie has a sweater on. Daddy, doggies don't wear sweaters. Why does that doggie have on a sweater?" Brooklyn looked up at her mommy and started to cry. She said to her mommy, "Doggies do wear sweaters. I wear them all the time. I have all colors of sweaters. Why did he say that, Mommy? Why doesn't he like my pretty sweater?" Brooklyn's mommy picked her up, rubbed her pretty little head and told her to stop crying. Her mommy told Brooklyn that little human children did not understand that doggies had to keep warm just as they did. Meanwhile, the little boy's father explained to him that doggies had to keep warm when it is cold outside the same way people do. Then the little boys ask Brooklyn's mommy if they could pet Brooklyn. She said, "Yes."

<u>The Walk Home Continued</u>

The older boy touched Brooklyn's head and said, "I love you, little doggie in your pretty sweater. I want to be your friend. My name is Billy." Brooklyn looked up at Billy and stopped crying. She said, "I forgive you. My name is Brooklyn, and I want to be your friend too." Ever since that special day, when Brooklyn and her mommy take their daily walks to the big park, she stops to play with her friend Billy, and he says, "Doggies do wear sweaters, because my friend Brooklyn wears all kinds of pretty sweaters all the time."

THE END!

About The Author

Shirley Lewis Larke is the author of this wonderful children's book. She was born in Wilmington Delaware, and currently resides there with her Doggie Brooklyn. She is the mother of three professional adults. These include Kim and Kevin (twins), and Braheem. She also has seven lovely grandchildren all of which she cherishes with all her heart. She is a God fearing woman and shows her dedication through her faith in her creator. She believes nothing is impossible with the help of her God. She has a BA in Human Service and Personnel Management, with a Master's (credits) in Special Education. She is an Educator, Entrepreneur and Counselor and now an Author. This is her first book… She gives praise to the one and only ADONAI *(The Lord, My Great Lord)*, for every area in her life and wholeheartedly humbles herself in his presence.

WARERESOURCES AND PUBLISHING
WE ARE AN ALL IN ONE,
ONE STOP PUBLISHING COMPANY!!!!

W.R.P. is a modest but skillful and knowledgeable Christian Publishing Company. We specialize in getting authors into print. We embrace and guide each author like a member of our family. We treat you fairly and recognize the importance of building a lasting relationship with you as an author. Join us in the walk to promote the message of encouragement and peace. Be one of the authors we help transform and prepare for the world of information and books.

FEEL FREE TO CONTACT US@
www.wareresources.com
1-800-469-4850 EXT. 2

http://www.facebook.com/pages/Ware-Resources-and-Publishing

www.ingramcontent.com/pod-product-compliance
Lightning Source LLC
Chambersburg PA
CBHW080927050426
42334CB00055B/2836